# HOW THE HUMAN BODY WORKS

# The Cardiovascular System

By Simon Rose

MEDIA ENHANCED BOOKS
AV²
BY WEIGL™
ADDED VALUE • AUDIO VISUAL

www.av2books.com

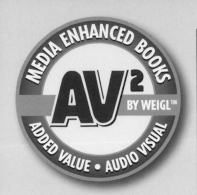

AV² provides enriched content that supplements and complements this book. Weigl's AV² books strive to create inspired learning and engage young minds in a total learning experience.

## Your AV² Media Enhanced books come alive with...

**Audio**
Listen to sections of the book read aloud.

**Key Words**
Study vocabulary, and complete a matching word activity.

**Video**
Watch informative video clips.

**Quizzes**
Test your knowledge.

**Embedded Weblinks**
Gain additional information for research.

**Slide Show**
View images and captions, and prepare a presentation.

Go to **www.av2books.com**, and enter this book's unique code.

## BOOK CODE

### M 5 6 9 3 4 6

**AV² by Weigl** brings you media enhanced books that support active learning.

**Try This!**
Complete activities and hands-on experiments.

## ... and much, much more!

Published by AV² by Weigl
350 5th Avenue, 59th Floor
New York, NY 10118
Websites: www.av2books.com   www.weigl.com

Library of Congress Cataloging-in-Publication Data Available on Request

ISBN 978-1-4896-1162-8 (hardcover)
ISBN 978-1-4896-1163-5 (softcover)
ISBN 978-1-4896-1164-2 (single-user eBook)
ISBN 978-1-4896-1165-9 (multi-user eBook)

Printed in the United States of America in North Mankato, Minnesota
1 2 3 4 5 6 7 8 9 0  18 17 16 15 14

062014
WEP090514

Project Coordinator  Aaron Carr
Art Director  Terry Paulhus

Photo Credits
Every reasonable effort has been made to trace ownership and to obtain permission to reprint copyright material. The publishers would be pleased to have any errors or omissions brought to their attention so that they may be corrected in subsequent printings.

Weigl acknowledges Getty Images as its primary image supplier for this title.

# Contents

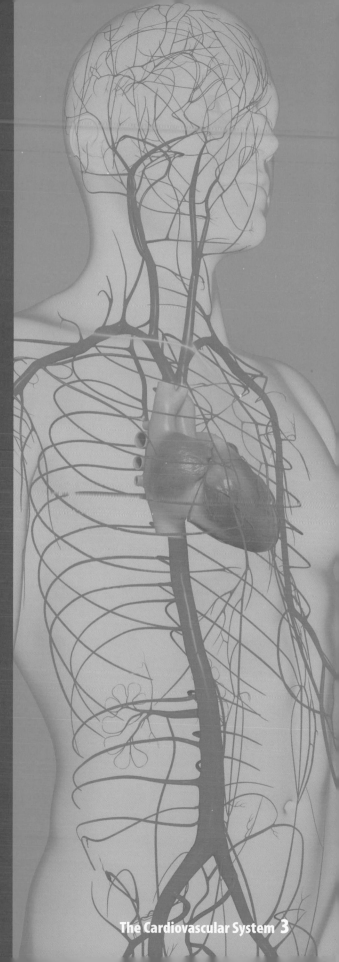

# Human Body Systems

The human body is made up of complex systems. Each one plays an important role in the operation of the body. The systems are also interconnected and work together to maintain **equilibrium**.

For the body to stay healthy, all of its systems need to work together properly. Problems or diseases that affect any of the body's systems can also cause problems in one or more others. Often, more severe conditions in one system affect a greater number of other systems.

## 6 MAJOR BODY SYSTEMS

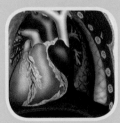

**CARDIOVASCULAR SYSTEM**

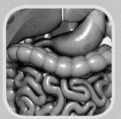

**DIGESTIVE SYSTEM**

**MUSCULAR SYSTEM**

**NERVOUS SYSTEM**

**RESPIRATORY SYSTEM**

**SKELETAL SYSTEM**

## CARDIOVASCULAR SYSTEM

Includes the heart and **blood vessels**

Contains about 11 pints (5 liters) of blood

Transports blood throughout the body

Is also known as the circulatory system

Provides the body with **nutrients**

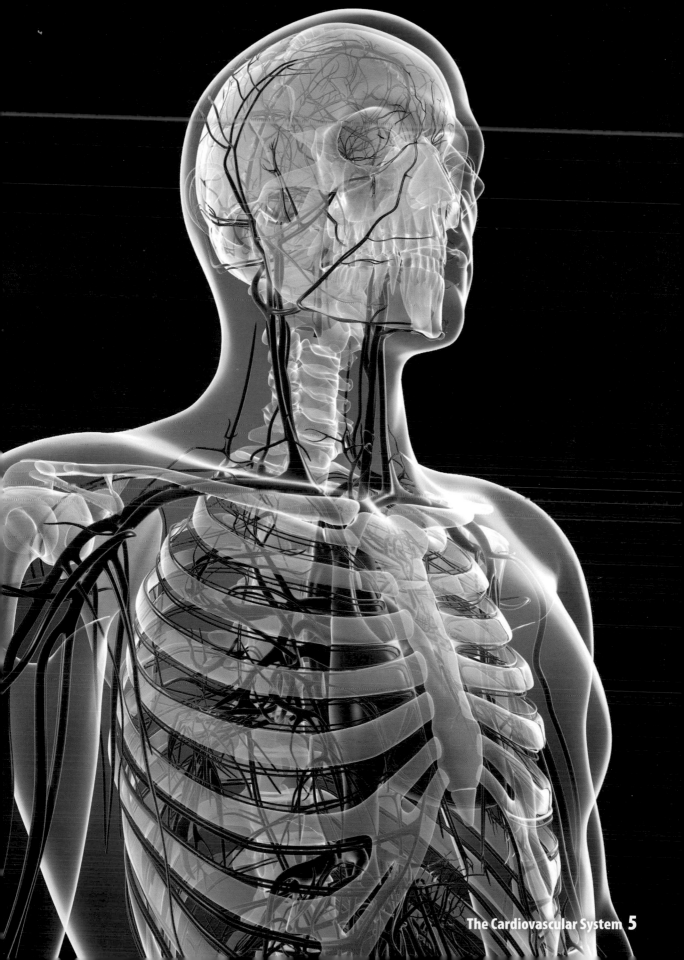

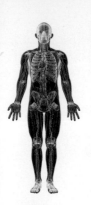

# What Is the Cardiovascular System?

**T**he cardiovascular system includes the heart and the body's blood vessels. The heart is one of the body's most important **organs**. It is connected to a network of blood vessels that deliver blood to other organs and **tissues**.

The heart acts like a pump, to send blood through the blood vessels. Blood transports **oxygen**, nutrients, and **hormones** throughout the body. In addition, the cardiovascular system helps rid the body of waste products. It works closely with the body's other systems to keep people healthy.

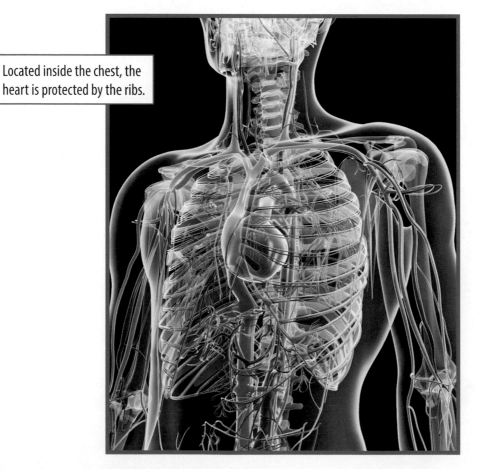

Located inside the chest, the heart is protected by the ribs.

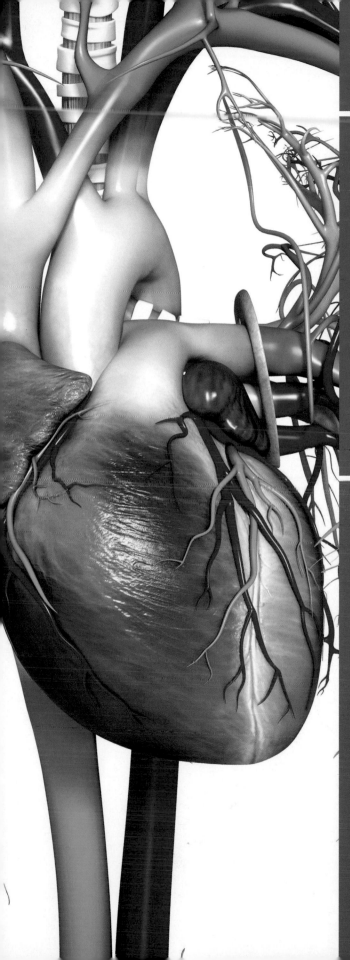

# 8–10 OUNCES (225–280 GRAMS) IS THE WEIGHT OF AN ADULT'S **HEART**.

To pump blood around the body, the heart beats about

# 70

times per minute.

There are **4** chambers, or sections, in the human heart.

Blood makes up **7%** of a person's body weight.

There are

# 60,000 MILES

(96,560 KILOMETERS) OF BLOOD VESSELS IN THE BODY.

When a person laughs, the heart pumps **20%** more blood.

# Cardiovascular System Features

The cardiovascular system includes three types of blood vessels. They are arteries, veins, and capillaries. Blood flows through the body in two circuits, or pathways, that begin and end at the heart. One is called the systemic circulation. It brings blood from the heart to most body organs and back again. The pulmonary circulation carries blood between the heart and the lungs.

**HEART** The heart is the main organ of the cardiovascular system.

**ARTERIES** Arteries are the vessels that carry blood away from the heart.

**VEINS** Veins carry blood back to the heart.

**CAPILLARIES** The smallest blood vessels, capillaries are located in most of the body's tissues and connect arteries to veins.

**AORTA** The largest artery in the body, the aorta connects the heart to other arteries.

**SUPERIOR AND INFERIOR VENAE CAVA** The superior and inferior venae cava are the two largest veins in the body.

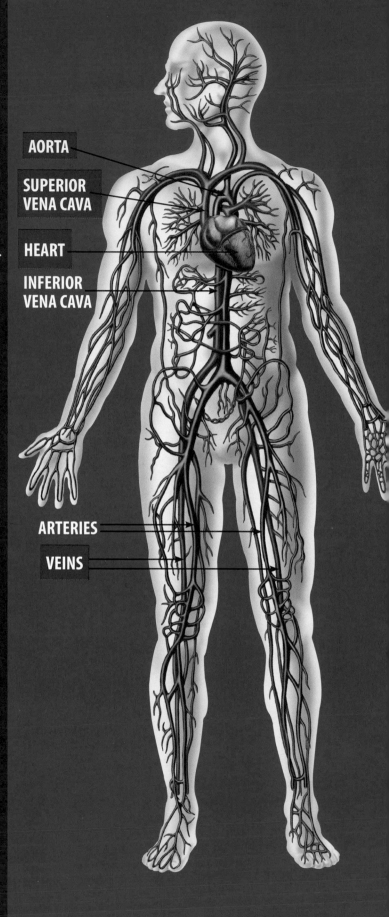

AORTA

SUPERIOR VENA CAVA

HEART

INFERIOR VENA CAVA

ARTERIES

VEINS

# HEART

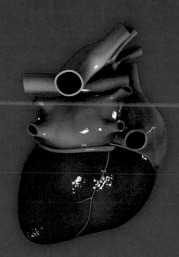

The heart is made of a type of muscle called cardiac muscle. This kind of muscle is found nowhere else in the body. The heart is hollow, so that it can receive and then send out blood.

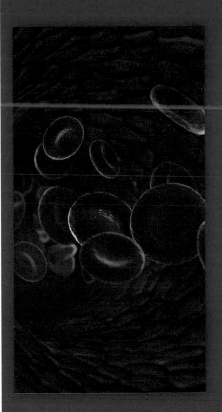

# ARTERIES AND VEINS

Arteries and veins contain layers of muscle and other types of tissue. Arteries are thicker and more rigid. Veins are thinner and more flexible. The smallest arteries are called arterioles. They connect to one end of capillaries. The other end of a capillary connects to a venule, which is a small vein.

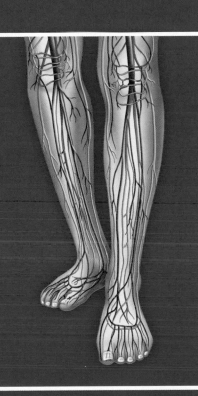

# BLOOD

Blood is the body's life fluid. The body's tissues and organs will stop functioning if they do not get a sufficient supply of blood to bring them substances they need and remove wastes.

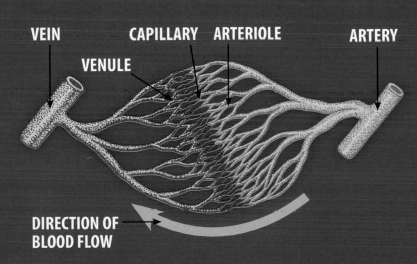

VEIN    CAPILLARY    ARTERIOLE    ARTERY

VENULE

**DIRECTION OF BLOOD FLOW**

# CAPILLARIES

The walls, or outsides, of capillaries are very thin. Nutrients and other substances the body needs pass through these walls to get from the blood to body tissues. Wastes, such as carbon dioxide gas, that tissues must get rid of also pass through capillary walls. They are then taken away by the blood.

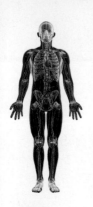

# How Does the Cardiovascular System Work?

The heart works constantly to pump blood throughout the body. The right side of the heart receives blood returning from most body organs and tissues. This returning blood contains very little oxygen. Most of the oxygen the blood carried was removed by body tissues to be used. The returning blood has carbon dioxide received from body tissues.

The heart sends this oxygen-poor blood to the lungs. When a person inhales, or breathes in, the lungs take in air that contains oxygen. In the lungs, the blood picks up oxygen that has been inhaled, and it transfers carbon dioxide to the lungs. The carbon dioxide is then removed from the body when a person exhales, or breathes out.

The blood leaving the lungs is now oxygen-rich, or well supplied with oxygen. This blood goes to the left side of the heart, which then pumps it out to travel through arteries to body tissues. The arteries expand and contract, or become wider and narrower. This pumping action by the arteries helps move blood through them. Blood in the arteries is a brighter red than blood returning to the heart in the veins. This is because oxygen combines with a substance in the blood called hemoglobin to give it a bright red color.

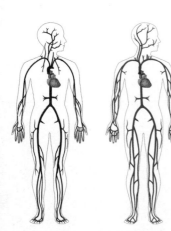

## The Role of the Cardiovascular System

**PROVIDE** Brings to the body's tissues substances they need in order to function.

**PROTECT** Helps the body fight infection.

**REMOVE** Helps the body get rid of wastes.

# Diagram of Blood Vessels and the Blood

Blood vessels have three layers. The inner layer is smooth. This allows blood to flow easily through the vessels. The middle layer is made up mostly of muscle. A tough outer layer protects blood vessels.

The content of the blood includes both liquid and solid substances. Plasma, which is made up mostly of water, is the liquid part of blood. Floating in the plasma are red blood cells, white blood cells, and platelets. Red blood cells, which contain hemoglobin, carry oxygen and carbon dioxide. White blood cells help the body fight infections and harmful substances. Platelets help the blood to clot at the site of a cut or other injury.

## Blood Vessels

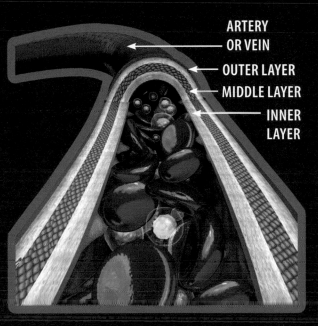

ARTERY OR VEIN

OUTER LAYER

MIDDLE LAYER

INNER LAYER

# 40%
of the blood is made up of red blood cells.

**A RED BLOOD CELL** lives for about 120 days, and the body is constantly making new ones to replace cells that die.

## Blood

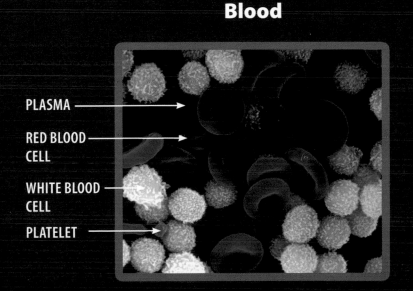

PLASMA

RED BLOOD CELL

WHITE BLOOD CELL

PLATELET

# The Heart

**T**he heart is located in the middle of the chest. A child's heart is around the same size as a fist. An adult's heart is about the size of two fists.

The heart's four chambers have thick, muscular walls. The upper section of the heart has two chambers, called the right atrium and left atrium. The atria receive blood that enters the heart from the veins. The lower part of the heart also has two chambers, called the right ventricle and left ventricle. These pump blood out of the heart into the arteries. There are four valves in the heart, located where blood leaves each chamber. The valves open to let blood out and then close again. This action keeps blood from flowing backward and makes sure that it is pumped in the right direction. Blood leaving the left ventricle enters the aorta, to be sent throughout the body.

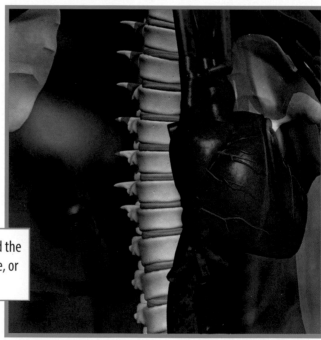

The heart is located toward the front of the body. The spine, or backbone, is behind it.

| The HEART by the Numbers | **0.4** | **2,000** | **100,000** |
|---|---|---|---|
| | The fraction of a second the heart rests between beats. | The number of gallons (7,570 liters) of blood pumped by an adult heart every day. | The number of times the heart beats per day. |

# Diagram of the Heart

About two-thirds of the heart is on the left side of the chest and one-third on the right side. The rate of a person's heartbeat depends on the body's activity. If a person is sitting still or sleeping, the heart will beat slowly. However, if a person is running, the heart beats faster to supply more oxygen to the muscles.

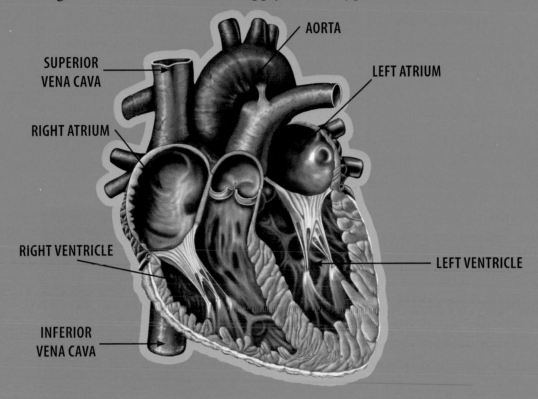

AORTA

SUPERIOR VENA CAVA

LEFT ATRIUM

RIGHT ATRIUM

RIGHT VENTRICLE

LEFT VENTRICLE

INFERIOR VENA CAVA

## HEART VALVES

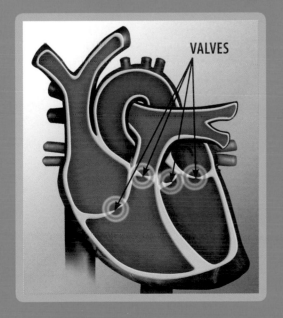

VALVES

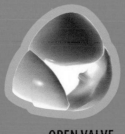

OPEN VALVE

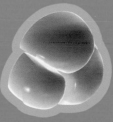

CLOSED VALVE

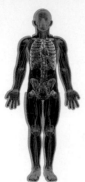

# The Body

In the head and neck, the arteries of the cardiovascular system send oxygen-rich blood to the brain. In the **torso**, the pulmonary arteries transport blood from the heart to the lungs. Other arteries in the torso bring blood to the organs of the digestive system, including the small intestine. Capillaries in the small intestine pick up nutrients from food the body has digested. The blood vessels then carry these nutrients to tissues throughout the body.

Blood traveling to the heart from the lungs is carried by the pulmonary veins to the left atrium. Blood returning from the upper body is brought by the superior vena cava to the right atrium, and blood from the lower body enters the right atrium from the inferior vena cava.

## Arms and Legs

Many different blood vessels carry blood through the arms and legs. All veins have valves to keep blood from flowing backward. These valves are especially important in leg veins, since the blood in these vessels has to travel the longest distance upward to reach the heart. If the valves do not close completely when they need to, a condition called varicose veins may result.

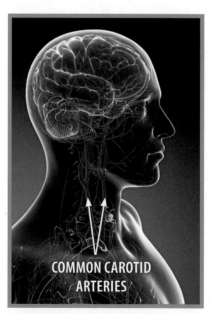

COMMON CAROTID ARTERIES

The common carotid arteries, one on each side of the neck, are the main vessels bringing blood to the brain and other parts of the head.

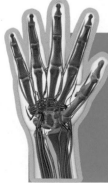

| The BODY'S BLOOD VESSELS by the Numbers | 15–20 | 2 | 20–25 |
|---|---|---|---|
| | Percentage of the body's blood supply that is used by the brain. | The number of arteries entering the hand. | Millions of Americans with varicose veins in their legs. |

# Diagrams of Arm and Leg Blood Vessels

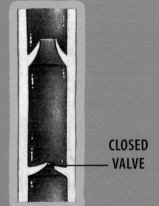

The flow of blood to the tissues of the arms and legs is very important to keep them healthy. Muscles in the arms need oxygen in order to function properly. Blood entering the arms from within the body is warm. Heat from the blood helps to protect the arms and especially the hands in cold weather. Blood flow reduces the risk of the fingers getting frostbite, or freezing.

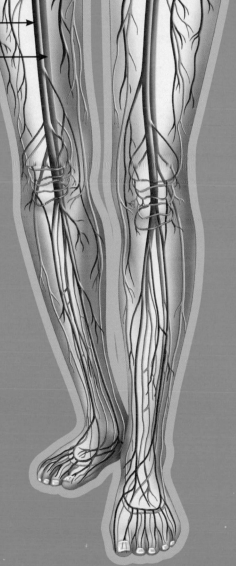

FEMORAL ARTERY

FEMORAL VEIN

The largest artery in each leg is the femoral artery, located in the thigh. It divides into several smaller arteries to supply blood to the lower leg and foot. In each leg, veins returning blood from the foot and lower leg combine to form the femoral vein.

**LEG VEIN VALVES** When a person has varicose veins, some blood may stay in the leg veins instead of moving upward. As a result, the veins swell. Varicose veins usually occur in the lower legs, ankles, and feet.

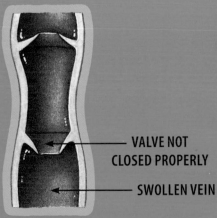

CLOSED VALVE

VALVE NOT CLOSED PROPERLY

SWOLLEN VEIN

# Blood Types

**E**veryone has blood, but blood is not the same in every person's body. There are four main types of blood. These are called A, B, AB, and O. All of these types have red and white blood cells, plasma, and platelets. The difference in blood types depends on whether the red blood cells have certain substances on them called antigens. These antigens, also known as markers, help in the process of fighting infections. There are A antigens and B antigens.

People with type A blood have A antigens on their red blood cells. In a person with type B blood, the red blood cells have B antigens. People with both A and B antigens on their red blood cells have type AB blood. Someone with type O blood has neither A nor B antigens on his or her red blood cells. No blood type is better for a person's health than any other.

## Rh Factor

Another antigen that some people have in their blood is called the Rhesus, or Rh, factor. People who have this marker are said to be Rh positive. Those who do not are Rh negative. People with each of the four main blood types may be either Rh positive or negative. For example, a person may be type A positive or type A negative.

Once the Rh classification is added to the main blood types, the number of blood types doubles to eight.

## BLOOD TYPES by the Numbers

**37%**
The portion of Americans who have type O positive blood.

**1%**
The percentage of Americans who have type AB negative blood.

**ABOUT 1/10**
The fraction of Americans with type B blood.

# Diagram of Blood Types

Blood type becomes an issue when a person needs a **blood transfusion**, because of an accident, during surgery, or as part of treatment for a disease. Then, it is very important for medical professionals to use only certain blood types with certain patients. Blood with certain markers cannot be given to people who have some blood types. For example, people with type A blood will become very ill and may even die if they receive a transfusion of type B blood.

**Donor**           **Recipient**

People with type O blood are known as universal donors because their blood can be given to anyone.

People with types A and AB can receive blood from type A donors.

Both types B and AB can receive blood from type B donors.

People with type AB can donate blood only to other ABs. They can receive any blood type.

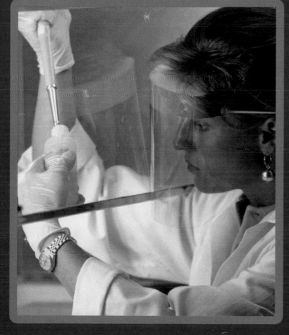

**TESTING BLOOD** All blood that is donated to be used for transfusions is tested many times by medical professionals. This testing makes sure that the blood type is correctly identified. Testing is also done to make sure that donated blood does not contain any disease-causing germs.

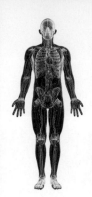

# Blood Pressure

**B**lood pressure is the pressure that the blood exerts on the walls of the blood vessels as it flows through them. Several factors determine a person's blood pressure. These include the strength of the heartbeat and how **elastic** the walls of the arteries are.

Doctors, nurses, or other medical professionals measure a person's blood pressure with a device called a sphygmomanometer. They wrap a cuff around the patient's upper arm. Air is pumped into the cuff, so that it squeezes the arm. Often, the health-care provider places a **stethoscope** over the inside of the patient's elbow. Air is then slowly let out of the cuff. As this occurs, the health-care provider listens to the blood flowing through a main artery, and the sphygmomanometer measures the changing pressure inside the artery.

A person's blood pressure measurement consists of two numbers. It is written as a fraction, such as 115/75. The first number is called the systolic pressure. It indicates pressure inside arteries when the heart is pumping blood. The second number is called the diastolic pressure. This indicates pressure in the arteries when the heart is resting between beats.

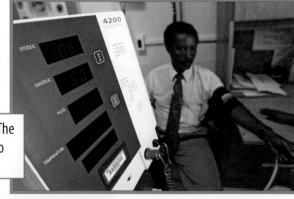

Some blood pressure devices are electronic. The reading is digital or signaled in beeps, and no stethoscope is used.

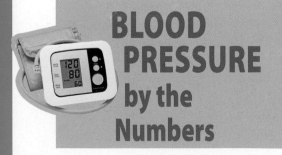

## BLOOD PRESSURE by the Numbers

| 76 | 2 | 27 |
|---|---|---|
| Millions of American adults with high blood pressure. | Adult should get a blood pressure check every two years. | Recent percentage increase in high blood pressure among children. |

# Facts about Blood Pressure

If a person's blood pressure is high, the heart is working too hard. This may mean that arteries have become too narrow or too stiff. Over time, high blood pressure, which is also called hypertension, can lead to severe health problems if it is not treated.

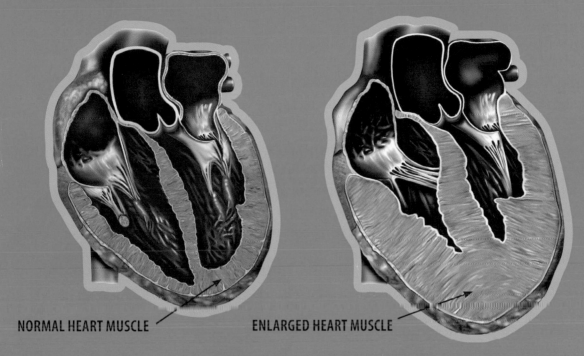

NORMAL HEART MUSCLE      ENLARGED HEART MUSCLE

When the heart works harder than it should, heart muscle can thicken and become too large. In time, an enlarged heart weakens and can fail.

| Blood Pressure Category | Systolic Pressure | Diastolic Pressure |
|---|---|---|
| Normal | less than 120 | less than 80 |
| Prehypertension | 120–139 | 80–89 |
| High Blood Pressure (Hypertension Stage 1) | 140–159 | 90–99 |
| High Blood Pressure (Hypertension Stage 2) | 160 or higher | 100 or higher |
| Hypertensive Crisis (Emergency care needed) | Higher than 180 | Higher than 110 |

Research has linked salt use to high blood pressure in some patients. However, salt may not be harmful for everyone.

There are several stages of hypertension. A person whose blood pressure is 180/110 or higher for a period of time should see a doctor as soon as possible.

# Keeping Healthy

The heart is vital to the health of the body. Therefore, it is important for people to take care of their cardiovascular systems. Eating the right foods, exercising, and keeping body weight at a healthful level are important.

## Healthful Foods

Eating foods that are low in fat helps the cardiovascular system stay healthy. These foods include fruits, vegetables, and whole-grain products such as bread, cereal, and pasta. Beans, chicken, and fish can be better food choices than red meats such as beef or lamb. Red meats tend to have more fat. Eating a great deal of fat can raise the amount in a person's blood of a substance called cholesterol. A high blood cholesterol level can increase the risk of heart disease.

## Exercise

Regular exercise increases the strength of the body's heart and lungs. As a result, the heart works less hard to pump blood. Exercise also helps avoid **obesity**, which increases the risk of heart disease.

Ideally, people should exercise for 60 minutes every day.

# FOOD FOR THE HEART

CHICKEN

BREAD

FRUIT

VEGETABLES

## Daily Habits

Over time, not getting enough sleep can increase both blood pressure and heartbeat rate. Research has shown that people who usually sleep for five hours or fewer each night have a higher risk of heart disease than those who get seven hours of sleep. Smoking is a habit that greatly increases a person's risk for many types of cardiovascular system diseases. Doctors recommend that people do not smoke.

# 500,000
**The number of American women who die each year from heart disease.**

# Heart Disease

There are several types of heart disease. One of the most common is atherosclerosis. In this condition, fatty deposits called plaque form on the inner walls of arteries, including the arteries that provide blood to the heart muscle. If the flow of blood to the heart muscle is blocked, the result is a **heart attack**.

PLAQUE

**Stroke** is a condition that often occurs when blood flow to the brain is blocked because of plaque in certain arteries.

# HIGH RISK
**Smoking is the NUMBER-ONE preventable cause of death in the world.**

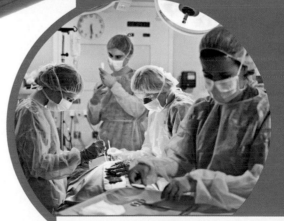

**Congenital heart defects** are present at birth. The most common type is a septal defect, or hole in the wall that separates two heart chambers. Doctors may try to close the hole with surgery.

# Studying the Cardiovascular System

Today, several types of medical professionals study and treat diseases of the cardiovascular system. However, people have been studying the human body and blood circulation since ancient times.

## UNDERSTANDING BLOOD FLOW

**1628** In England, William Harvey first describes blood circulation and how the heart pumps blood around the body.

**About 600 BC**

Indian physician Sushruta describes how vital fluids circulate in the human body.

**About 200 AD**

The Greek physician Galen distinguishes between veins and arteries.

F. John Lewis performs the world's first successful open heart surgery, or operation on the heart in which the patient's chest is cut open.

**1952**

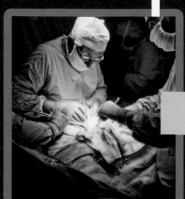

Christiaan Barnard of South Africa performs the first heart **transplant** surgery.

**1967**

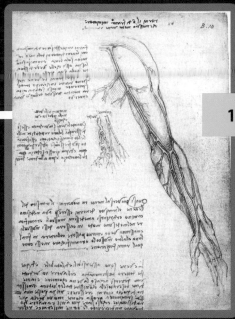

**1510**

Italian artist and scientist Leonardo da Vinci is the first person to draw an accurate sketch of the human heart and blood vessels.

Raymond de Vieussens of France relates symptoms of heart disease to problems in specific parts of the cardiovascular system.

**1715**

**1832**

The Anatomy Act in Great Britain regulates the supply of dead bodies for medical research.

**1733**

Stephen Hales measures human blood pressure for the first time.

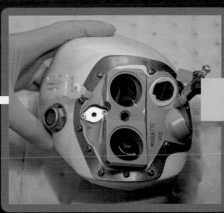

**1982**

Robert Jarvik designs the first artificial heart, which is placed in a patient by surgeon William DeVries.

**2013**

The first artificial heart that contracts like a human heart is developed.

# Working Together

**N**o system in the human body works alone. All the systems must work together to keep people healthy. The cardiovascular system works closely with several other systems in the body.

## Blood Vessels and Lymph Vessels

The cardiovascular and lymphatic systems are connected. The lymphatic system includes tube-like vessels similar to blood vessels. Plasma that seeps through capillaries into body tissues is collected by the lymphatic system. This liquid then flows through the lymph vessels to be returned to the blood. In this way, the lymphatic system makes sure the blood contains enough liquid.

Several types of white blood cells mature, or develop, in the lymphatic system. These cells then enter the blood to be transported around the body. A lymphatic system organ called the spleen cleans the blood.

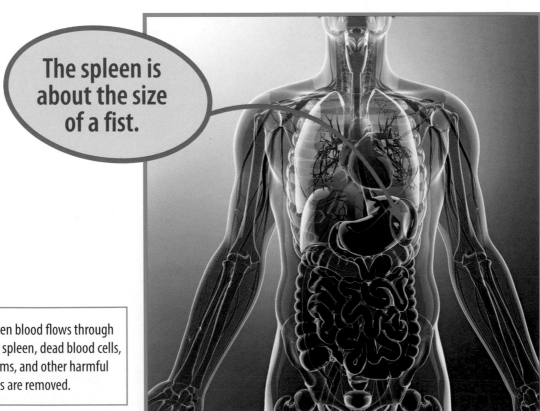

The spleen is about the size of a fist.

When blood flows through the spleen, dead blood cells, germs, and other harmful cells are removed.

## Blood Cells and Bones

The cardiovascular system's red blood cells are made in the skeletal system. They are produced in the soft substance called marrow that is inside bones. White blood cells are also made in the bone marrow before maturing in the lymphatic system.

## Blood and Hormones

The endocrine system produces hormones that the blood carries throughout the body. There are many types of hormones, which have different functions. For example, the hormone insulin regulates the amount of sugar in the blood.

In the early 1900s, Canadian scientists Frederick Banting and Charles Herbert Best made important discoveries about insulin.

# More Than One

The kidneys are two organs of the excretory system. They remove from the blood many of the wastes that the blood picks up from body tissues. These substances then leave the body before they can build up to harmful levels.

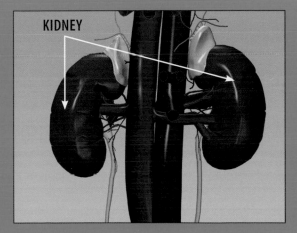

KIDNEY

# Careers

Several careers in health care involve working with patients who have cardiovascular system problems. Before considering a career, it is important to research options and learn about the educational requirements. It is also important to understand what the day-to-day work involves.

## Cardiologist

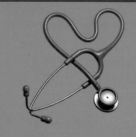
Cardiologists specialize in diagnosing and treating diseases of the heart and other parts of the cardiovascular system. They also advise patients about changes in diet, exercise, and other habits to control or reverse some conditions. Cardiologists work closely with cardiovascular surgeons, deciding if a patient needs surgery. A cardiologist's patients can include children with heart conditions from birth, as well as adults of all ages with heart diseases.

## Education

Cardiologists usually obtain a bachelor's degree in some area of science. After college, they attend medical school for four years. Following medical school, they receive advanced training in **residency** programs.

A cardiovascular surgeon, also known as a heart surgeon, operates on the heart or blood vessels. A common type of heart surgery involves replacing heart valves that are not functioning properly. Cardiovascular surgeons also operate to remove plaque from arteries or to widen narrowed arteries using a balloon-like device.

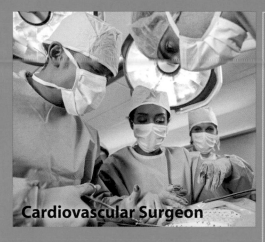
Cardiovascular Surgeon

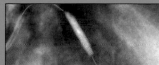

### Education
- Four years of medical school
- Three-year residency in general surgery
- Three-year residency in cardiovascular surgery

### Tools
Angioplasty balloon

## Education
A bachelor's degree is required. After college, cardiovascular surgeons attend medical school. Their residency programs after medical school train them to become surgeons.

Paramedics and emergency medical technicians (EMTs) are often the first medical professionals on the scene if a patient has a heart attack. Paramedics have training that allows them to give more advanced care than EMTs. Both provide emergency care and get the patient safely to a hospital. On occasion, they use a device called a defibrillator to restore a patient's heartbeat with a controlled electric shock.

Paramedic/EMT

### Education
- High school degree
- EMT-Basic, EMT-Intermediate, and Paramedic training programs
- Must pass an examination to become certified

### Tools

Defibrillator

## Education
Most paramedics and EMTs have graduated from high school. They then take training programs to prepare them for their job. There are two levels of training for EMTs. Paramedics complete both of these and then take higher-level training.

# The Cardiovascular System Quiz

Test your knowledge of the cardiovascular system by answering these questions. The answers are provided below for easy reference.

**1** What is the main organ of the cardiovascular system?

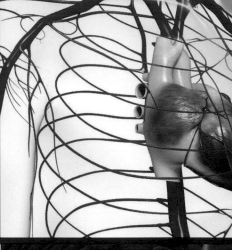

**1** What is the main organ of the cardiovascular system?

**4** For about how many days will a red blood cell circulate around the body?

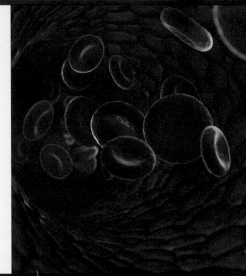

**7** What is the total length of all the blood vessels in the human body?

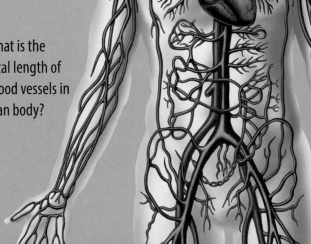

**9** What are the four main blood types?

## ANSWER KEY

**10** The pulmonary arteries
**9** A, B, AB, and 0
**8** Capillaries
**7** 60,000 miles (96,560 km)
**6** The aorta
**5** Smoking
**4** 120
**3** Christiaan Barnard
**2** Hypertension
**1** The heart

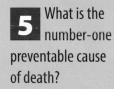

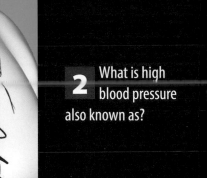

**2** What is high blood pressure also known as?

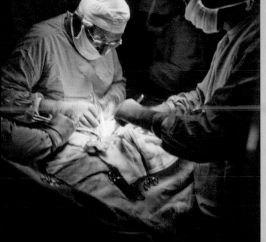

**3** Who performed the first heart transplant surgery in 1967?

**5** What is the number-one preventable cause of death?

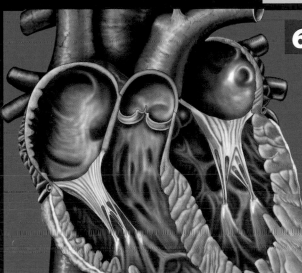

**6** What is the largest artery in the body?

**8** What type of blood vessels connect arterioles and venules?

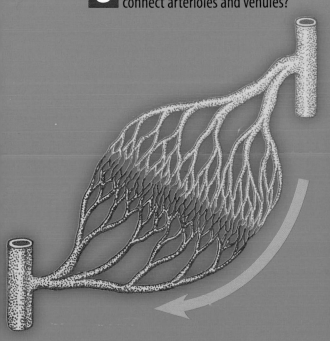

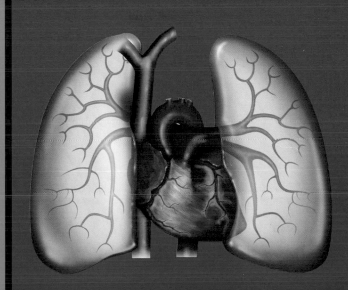

**10** Which blood vessels carry blood from the heart to the lungs?

# Activity

The sound of the heart beating is often described as lub-DUB, lub-DUB, lub-DUB. This sound is made when heart valves open and close as the heart pumps blood. Medical professionals use a stethoscope to hear the heart beating. Complete this activity with a partner to make your own stethoscope and determine your heartbeat rates.

Hearing Your Heart

## BEFORE YOU START, YOU WILL NEED:

- 1 empty paper towel roll
- 1 plastic funnel
- 6-inch (15-centimeter) strip of duct tape
- 1 chart with 2 columns for student names and 2 rows for Resting and Exercising

**1** Place the narrow part of the funnel into one end of the tube-shaped paper towel roll. Tape the funnel to the tube with the duct tape. Use this home-made stethoscope to listen to each other's heartbeats.

**2** Place the funnel on your partner's chest, slightly to the left of center. Place the other end of the tube by your ear.

**3** Count the number of heartbeats for 20 seconds. Then, multiply that number by 3 to obtain the number of beats per minute.

**4** Record your partner's heartbeats per minute in the Resting column of the chart.

**5** After your partner does about 2 minutes of vigorous exercise, such as running in place or jumping jacks, measure and record the heartbeats again, this time in the Exercising column.

**6** Repeat Steps 2 through 5, this time with your partner measuring and recording your heartbeats.

**7** How did your heartbeat rates change after exercising? Why did this change occur?

# Key Words

**blood transfusion**: when a person receives blood that was donated by someone else

**blood vessels**: tube-shaped structures that carry blood around the body

**elastic**: able to stretch and then return to its original shape

**equilibrium**: a state of balance, such as when parts of the body work properly together

**heart attack**: the death of, or damage to, part of the heart muscle because the supply of blood is greatly reduced or stopped

**hormones**: substances in the body that influence the way the body grows and functions

**nutrients**: substances that are needed by the body to stay healthy

**obesity**: when a person is extremely overweight

**organs**: parts of the body that perform special functions

**oxygen**: a gas that is found in air and that is essential for body tissues to function properly

**residency**: the period when a medical professional trains in a specialized field by practicing under the supervision of more experienced doctors

**stethoscope**: a medical instrument used to listen to sounds inside a patient's body

**tissues**: structures in the body made up of the same type of cells, which are the smallest units in living things that can perform the functions necessary for life

**torso**: the main part of the body, not including the head, neck, arms, and legs

**transplant**: a type of surgery in which an organ from one person is placed in another person's body

# Index

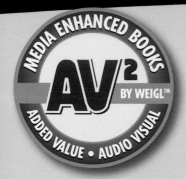

# Log on to www.av2books.com

AV² by Weigl brings you media enhanced books that support active learning. Go to www.av2books.com, and enter the special code found on page 2 of this book. You will gain access to enriched and enhanced content that supplements and complements this book. Content includes video, audio, weblinks, quizzes, a slide show, and activities.

## AV² Online Navigation

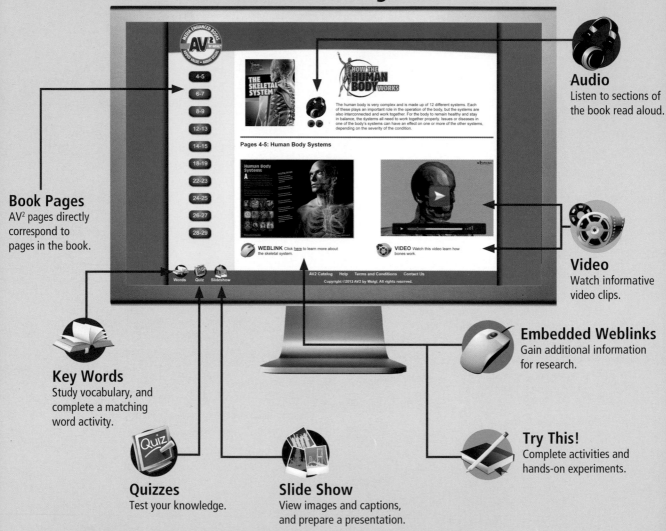

**Audio**
Listen to sections of the book read aloud.

**Book Pages**
AV² pages directly correspond to pages in the book.

**Video**
Watch informative video clips.

**Embedded Weblinks**
Gain additional information for research.

**Key Words**
Study vocabulary, and complete a matching word activity.

**Try This!**
Complete activities and hands-on experiments.

**Quizzes**
Test your knowledge.

**Slide Show**
View images and captions, and prepare a presentation.

---

AV² was built to bridge the gap between print and digital. We encourage you to tell us what you like and what you want to see in the future.

## Sign up to be an AV² Ambassador at www.av2books.com/ambassador.

Due to the dynamic nature of the Internet, some of the URLs and activities provided as part of AV² by Weigl may have changed or ceased to exist. AV² by Weigl accepts no responsibility for any such changes. All media enhanced books are regularly monitored to update addresses and sites in a timely manner. Contact AV² by Weigl at 1-866-649-3445 or av2books@weigl.com with any questions, comments, or feedback.